Fast Track to Business Excellence

Outstanding Leadership

Fast Track to Business Excellence

Other books in the series:

Exceptional Entrepreneurship

Managing Your People

Mastering Change

Fast Track to Business Excellence

Outstanding Leadership

Real-Life Lessons from Top Business Leaders

Adapted from the Fifty Lessons
Digital Video Library

GLOBAL
professional
publishing

This edition published by
Global Professional Publishing Limited
The European Innovation Centre
Fitzroy House
11 Chenies Street
London WC1E 7EY

ISBN: 9780852976531

Typeset by Kevin O'Connor

Printed and bound in Great Britain by
Presstige Communications

Set in Clarendon Light and Scala sans

Contents

Acknowledgements

We would like to thank all of the executives who have contributed their hard-won lessons to the Fifty Lessons Digital Video Library from which the *Fast Track to Business Excellence* books are derived.

Recording the first-hand learning experiences of today's business leaders will prove of immeasurable value to the business leaders of the future.

About Fifty Lessons

Wherever you are on the career ladder, you are walking in the footsteps of others. Whatever business dilemma you are facing, some of the finest brains in business have faced it before.

Fifty Lessons was born out of a desire to learn from the experience of today's greatest business minds. They felt that decades of hard-won business experience were being written off to the vagaries of memory and resolved to capture, store and pass on this wisdom to the next generation.

Using the power of storytelling, they have captured on film the most valuable and defining experiences of some of the biggest names in international business, and built them into a digital library containing over 700 lessons.

The *Fast Track to Business Excellence* series features specially chosen lessons from this library, offering inspiration, practical help and guidance across a diverse range of management challenges. In business, as in life, learning from the knowledge of others is invaluable. There is no substitute for experience.

For access to filmed interviews from the entire Fifty Lessons Digital Video Library, please visit: www.fiftylessons.com/fasttrack

Introduction to Outstanding Leadership

An outstanding business needs to encourage outstanding leadership. With it comes effective communication, improved performance and business growth. Without it an organization will drift or fracture, allowing the competition to gain the advantage.

Outstanding Leadership gives you access to the real-life business experience of twelve exceptional business leaders in a pocket-sized format. Their personal stories, and how they learnt from their experiences, provide winning strategies and a fast track to understanding the best approaches to leadership.

The book begins with the need to take responsibility for the actions of the organization, to eliminate a blame culture, and to set clear goals for people to buy into and follow. Core characteristics of leadership include a talent for perseverance, a willingness to be visible and to lead from the front, and having the courage of your convictions. The book ends on the importance of understanding and appreciating the value of people and their expertise. True leadership ability is a rare asset and it should be nurtured at all costs.

Whatever your level of management experience, these personal stories provide invaluable knowledge, insight and understanding of how best to be an outstanding leader.

Responsibility lies ultimately with the company's Chief Executive. Being in charge means just that; people should not blame subordinates or try to pass the buck.

1a Eliminate Blame

Domenico De Sole

Former President & CEO, *Gucci Group*

My Career

“I was born in Rome in 1944. After leaving school, I studied for a law degree, and in 1970 decided to move to the United States to study for my Masters Degree at Harvard University. Upon graduation, I practised law and then became a partner in the Washington law firm of Patton, Boggs & Blow.

My career at Gucci began in 1984, when I joined the company as Chief Executive Officer of Gucci America. I remained in New York until 1994, but then moved to Italy to take up my role as the Group's Chief Operating Officer. I was appointed President and CEO of Gucci Group NV the following year, and became Chairman of the Group's Management Board.

During this time I worked hard to re-establish the exclusivity and profitability of the Gucci brand, which we achieved by focusing on Gucci's core leather products and investing in advertising and communication, as well as in men's clothing and women's ready-to-wear fashion. Important elements of this strategy included the strengthening of the company's information and logistics processes, improving efficiency, and upgrading and expanding the network of directly operated stores.

At the end of 1995 Gucci Group NV was listed on the New York and Amsterdam stock exchanges. This was followed in 1997 by the purchase of Gucci's Timepieces, the company's most important licence. In 1999 we successfully fought a hostile takeover bid, and the outcome further enhanced shareholder value. In the same year we also began a new phase of acquisition: Gucci completed the purchase of Yves Saint Laurent, Sanofi Beauté (now YSL Beauté) and Sergio Rossi; in 2000 we acquired Boucheron, Alexander McQueen and Bedat & Co, and in 2001 Bottega Veneta, Stella McCartney and Balenciaga SA, owner of the Balenciaga luxury brand.

One of the most pleasing outcomes for me is that during my time leading the Gucci Group we went from bankruptcy in 1994 to being the third largest – and one of the most profitable – luxury multi-brand companies in the world. At the end of April 2004 the Gucci Group's largest shareholder, the French retail group Pinault Printemps Redoute, took complete control. I retired from my role within Gucci soon afterwards, and I am now a Director of Procter & Gamble, as well as a Director of Gap Inc, Bausch & Lomb, and Telecom Italia.

Domenico De Sole

Former President & CEO, *Gucci Group*

Domenico De Sole was a Director of Procter & Gamble until 2005. In addition to his other Directorships, he is now a Director of Delta Air Lines.

Eliminate Blame

The manager or the CEO is always responsible. This great principle is incredibly important for good management. I remember that Maurizio Gucci, the former CEO and the last family member to manage the company, was always critical of his organization. The thing that struck me as really bizarre was that he was always blaming somebody else for its problems. If a collection was not very good, he would blame his designer; then he would complain about stores not displaying the collection on time, being late, or pricing too expensively. Then he would blame the creative director who developed the store. We were talking about it one day and finally I said, 'But Maurizio, you are the CEO – you run the company. How can you blame everybody else for everything that goes wrong in the company? You are in charge. You are responsible. If you don't think these people know what they are doing, you should fire them – but if they are there because you trust and value them, then it's up to you to make sure that they execute their responsibilities properly.'

Unfortunately, I see this habit in a lot of companies. People try to blame subordinates. I think blaming subordinates is silly. Either you're in charge or you're not in charge. If you are the person who makes the final decisions, and you are the person who appoints the other people, then in the end you are responsible. I always say jokingly that in my company if the fashion show is great, the designer takes all the credit. If the fashion show is bad, it's my fault. At the end he – and everybody else – reports to me, so the CEO must take responsibility.

Domenico De Sole

Typically, CEOs who are not very good will always look for who did it.

I really think the best thing you learn in business is that you make mistakes. Everybody makes mistakes, and the people in charge must be in charge and take responsibility for failure, even taking responsibility for the failure to supervise somebody else – so there really is no excuse. Typically, CEOs who are not very good will always look for who did it. They will try to find a culprit. I really do believe that that is irrelevant. If a mistake has been made, the responsibility must be assumed at the management level, then the situation should be moved forward to understand why the mistake was made in order to avoid the same mistake being made twice.

I have never blamed anybody else in my life, but the corollary of this is that I do expect performance from people. I need them to understand that if they're in charge, they're in charge. They are responsible for producing the results and for making sure that everything gets done properly.

The senior management sets the culture and tone of an organization. It should lead by example, and through personal commitment energize the team and ensure that everyone understands and responds to the identified goals.

1b The CEO Sets the Tone

A mission statement should be clear and repeated regularly.

It is totally clear to me that any company wanting to be successful must have a very precise sense of its mission: it must know where it is going and how it plans to get from A to B. Most importantly, the manager must set the tone of the mission. That is critical. Each layer of management, whether at senior or middle level, needs to understand what the mission is, what the company is trying to achieve, and what the goals of the company are. These goals must be very clear, simple and expressed in a way that makes them easily understood. What I say to everybody is that a mission statement should be clear and repeated regularly.

It is important for a CEO to keep repeating the same basic principle in order to make sure that everybody at every level of the organization commits to the mission, shares the dream and understands what needs to be done. By the same token, I am a true believer that senior management must set the tone, and that begins with the CEO. For example, it is very difficult to say to people that they have to save money if there is a management style in place that is wasteful. That is true for everything. It's difficult to create a culture of hard work and responsibility if there is no culture of hard work at the CEO level.

When I went to Italy back in 1993 or 1994 my immediate priority was to get everybody in agreement about the internal mission, to understand what we were trying to do and to start executing it properly. I used to be there all the time. I would arrive at the crack of dawn and still be there very late every night; I would work on weekends, and I would call people all the time and at any time. When I said that something needed to be done, I would keep following up and calling back, asking: 'Has it been done?' I was very visible. I was living in Florence at the time and visiting all our suppliers in the area, so I had a very strong presence within the organization and made sure that everybody communicated with me; but, importantly, I also used to communicate with them. At that time I had more people reporting to me and the company was smaller, but the sense that things were going to change and that things needed to be done was very strong. They saw me working full time.

Luxury companies are very strong in Asia, so I started travelling there too – constantly – because I recognized that this was an important market for us to grow. Again, I established a very strong presence and demonstrated to a lot of people that there was very strong personal commitment on my part.

I really do feel that one of the most important tenets for a CEO or a manager is to make sure that everybody views you as a person who practises what he preaches. You have to set the tone, be the leader and set the example. Second, it is important that the mission is stated simply, clearly and repeated at regular intervals to make sure that it filters through the entire organization, and everybody really understands the goal of the company, what it is trying to achieve and how to get there. ”

Executive Timeline Domenico De Sole

1970	Moved from Italy to the USA.
Early years	Masters Degree – Harvard University
	Patton, Boggs & Blow *Partner* Patton, Boggs & Blow is a Washington law firm.
1984	**Gucci** Joined what has become one of the world's leading multi-brand companies in the luxury goods market.
1984–1994	**Gucci America Inc** *Chief Executive Officer*
1994	**Gucci Group NV** *Group Chief Operating Officer*
	Moved to Italy.
1995	Led Gucci Group NV's listing on the New York and Amsterdam stock exchanges.
1999	Successfully fought a hostile takeover bid, securing Gucci's independence as a basis for continued expansion, including the acquisition of Yves Saint Laurent, Alexander McQueen and Stella McCartney.
1995–2004	*President and Chief Executive Officer*
2001–2005	**Procter & Gamble**, Cincinnati *Director* P&G is a leading manufacturer of consumer health and beauty products.
2005–present	**Delta Air Lines**, Atlanta *Director*

Every leader has a responsibility to set the right tone at the top. To live the values the company espouses and to lead by example; just repeating the rhetoric is not enough.

2a Setting the Right Tone at the Top

Sir Michael Rake

Chairman, *KPMG International*

"My career has been interesting. I became an accountant very reluctantly at a time when I decided the UK was going down the drain. I wanted to qualify and leave the country, and thought the best way to do this was to become a Chartered Accountant. I qualified in the UK, then left immediately for Belgium with the firm I was articled to at the time. I spent the next fourteen years in Continental Europe, and ended up running their audit business in Belgium and Luxembourg. I transferred in 1974 to what was then Peat Marwick. I moved to run the Middle East practice from 1986 to 1989, before briefly running the Belgium practice, and then returning to the UK to become a Board Member. I had various major international clients and held various management positions within the UK. I was elected UK Senior Partner in 1998, European Chairman in 1999, and Global Chairman in 2002.

Sir Michael Rake

Chairman, *KPMG International*

The tone that an individual leader sets is the most important in influencing the way that the organization works as a whole.

In the past few years a complete breakdown in trust has developed in the business world. There has been a breakdown in trust in the operation of the capital markets, in the trust of chief executives and the way they operate, and there is an assumption that everyone operates out of a sense of greed, if not dishonesty, enriching themselves at the expense of others. This is one of the results of the impact of recent corporate scandals not only in the United States, but also in the UK. As a consequence, we've seen the evolution of an enormous amount of regulation, legislation, litigation and rule-making. Yet, for me, the reason we've had these problems and these cases of extreme behaviour and extreme greed relates to the underlying culture of an organization.

Things can go wrong from operational and environmental points of view, but if you examine corporate culture, you often find that it's the tone at the top, the tone that an individual leader sets, that is most important in influencing the way an organization works as a whole. We need to understand the importance of this issue when we take responsibility for public companies, whether as advisers, auditors, or as Non-executive Directors, because if the leadership doesn't set the right tone, it's amazing how even intelligent people become overwhelmed by the prevailing culture. That was clearly the case in Enron, and has clearly been the case in many other companies where the culture went wrong at the top.

This introduces the real issue of leadership by example, because one of the key things leaders have to understand is that they're extremely visible. Anything they do is exaggerated when communicated across the company, so their attitude towards life, their basic values and what they say are very important. How do managers behave towards other people? Do they have a sense of integrity? What degree of respect do they hold for other people within the organization, whatever their level, and is it genuine respect rather than paying lip-service to a charter? Enron had a laudable charter of values in Corporate Social Responsibility (CSR), but underneath it was almost a smokescreen for abuse.

Organizations need a corporate culture where people can see that the values go beyond rhetoric, beyond a charter of values, and that the ethos is sincere – people at the top really live the values of the organization. The reason companies endorse concepts like CSR is that they are incredibly important to the corporate reputation; such concepts are not only the right thing for the communities that businesses operate within, but the business case is enormously important too. CSR enables a company to portray a positive image to the outside world. It adds value to its brand, it adds prestige and pride to its people, it aids recruitment and retention, and it also creates the right culture within a capitalist world.

Capitalism and public companies: the only reason we have them is so that they create wealth for many rather than just a few. For that premise to be trusted, and to be seen and believed in by employees, regulators, politicians and journalists, the company has to act upon its principles: it has to deliver and live by them. In my experience, for this to work it always begins by the person at the top setting the example.

What is striking in investigations that KPMG has done into companies and individuals where things have gone wrong is that often we find that the individuals involved don't realize that they have committed an illegal act. They have crossed the line, if you like, from white to grey to black. Where the organizational culture has gone wrong, or the tone at the top is wrong, most of them have had to operate within the grey area for a lot of the time. Therefore, when they cross into the black area and actually commit an illegal and criminal act, they don't realize that they have crossed that line. When you interview these individuals you find that because the culture of the organization has gone wrong, and because of the aggressiveness with which the targets are set, or the ways in which their achievement of those targets is rewarded, intelligent and innately honest people suddenly think that their actions are acceptable, because within that environment they seem to be okay. However they are not okay, and they've done something that is illegal, immoral or criminal.

Organizations and leaders need to create an environment that actually rewards the right culture. People who are

> Where the organizational culture has gone wrong, people have had to operate within a grey area ... when they commit a criminal act, they don't realize they have crossed a line.

promoted into management roles need to be role models and seen to be people who demonstrate corporate values and integrity of approach. People who have been properly counselled or advised and who still do not adopt the corporate values need to be dealt with. However clever or technically brilliant they might be, if they're creating an environment where the culture is wrong, they're going to be a net deficit to the organization. Management needs to think seriously about removing them, because such behaviour is pernicious, and destructive attitudes can spread, creating an environment where people think that you have to behave in an inappropriate way in order to survive or succeed. It's very damaging for an organization. Not every case ends like Enron, but in a lot of companies that fail or become inefficient due to an unhealthy corporate culture, the people have become demotivated. In a large organization you have to work very hard to ensure that people understand the corporate values and the way they as individuals should operate.

The basic lesson is that it is the responsibility of any leader to set the right tone at the top, to live the values that the company espouses and to lead by example.

Learn to be self-reliant and resilient from a young age; there will always be unexpected issues to face, and as a leader you need continuously to project confidence so that your people trust in your ability to find the solution.

2b The Self-reliant Leader

I was fortunate in that I learnt how to be self-reliant and resilient very early on in my management experience. It is critically important to learn these skills young, otherwise, when you reach the top of an organization, particularly a large one, you may find yourself in quite a lonely position. When you are at the top you need continuously to project confidence, you need to reflect something that your people understand and have confidence in.

For me, learning these lessons goes back to 1986, when I was asked by KPMG to go to the Middle East. It was the time of the Iran/Iraq war and there were huge financial crises occurring in the banking sector in the region. We had a lot of difficulties in our business there: two or three of our people were under investigation by the judicial authorities; we didn't have enough cash to pay the wages at the end of the month; and, I think the day after I'd been told that, we lost a client that was worth about 30 per cent of our revenues. I remember calling my boss in London to let him know and he said: 'Well, good luck, Mike!' It was a very good lesson for me.

We went from near collapse and catastrophe to assembling a group of people who realized we had to deal with the situation. We not only dealt with the immediate issues, but also within the next very difficult two years we recovered our market position, were highly profitable, were remitting profits back to the head office, and people were willing and keen to join us. Our reputation had been fully re-established.

One needed to be pretty tough in confronting the situation, recognizing that one had no choice but to get on with it, to ensure that people had some confidence – even though I wasn't quite sure what on earth I was going to do to resolve matters. I think the fact that people had confidence meant that the team really pulled together. There was a realization that together we had to find a solution because no one was going to help us, so we might as well get out there and do something about it. That gave us the impetus to fight back.

It appeared at the beginning that everything was against us, but step by step we dealt with one thing, then another, then another; and we found that if we worked hard enough at it, we suddenly got a bit of good luck too, and events started to go in the right direction. Learning to deal with each and every issue, learning that there is no escape but to deal with them yourself, realizing that you have to motivate people to work with you to find solutions, and being absolutely determined because you have no choice, are enormously important lessons. The younger you learn them, the better for you.

It comes down to understanding how an individual and an organization interrelate. If people understand that, they will be given some authority with responsibility. People need to understand that if they make a decision and it's the right one, they will get credit for it, but what they will never be allowed to do is make no decision and pass it to somebody else.

Step by step we dealt with one thing, then another, then another; and we found that if we worked hard enough at it, we suddenly got a bit of good luck too, and events started to go in the right direction.

There are some people in senior positions who love to make all the decisions, so to some extent they create an environment of dependence. Whilst they must be resilient and self-reliant, leaders should not plan or expect to make every decision, because if they do, the result will be that every decision is pushed in their direction for them to make, and no one else in the organization will make decisions. There will be sclerosis of the organization, stemming from the top, because everything has to come from one person. This situation needs to be avoided. It's characteristic of what you'd call a 'control freak' in a command-and-control environment. In an empowered environment, where people can deal with issues, they will come up with solutions and implement them, knowing they won't always get it right, but knowing they're expected to do something to make a difference, and to deal with the issues they face.

When in a leadership position, it is important to ensure that the people whom you are developing within the organization are given the opportunity to gain experience where they have to be self-reliant and learn to handle issues. Everybody knows, in whatever business they are in – whether running a medical practice, an accounting practice, or a FTSE 100 company – that there are times when you get bad news and things go wrong. Learning to deal with bad news is critical, as is the ability to turn it round, and ask: 'What can I do?', 'What are the good things?' and 'What are the silver linings within that particular cloud?'

People need to understand that if they make a decision and it's the right one, they will get credit for it, but what they will never be allowed to do is make no decision and pass it to somebody else.

How you react to each situation is critically important to the people around you, to how the organization sees you, and therefore to how the organization responds to that particular crisis. If you start getting downcast or depressed, you will have grave difficulty in bringing your people with you. ”

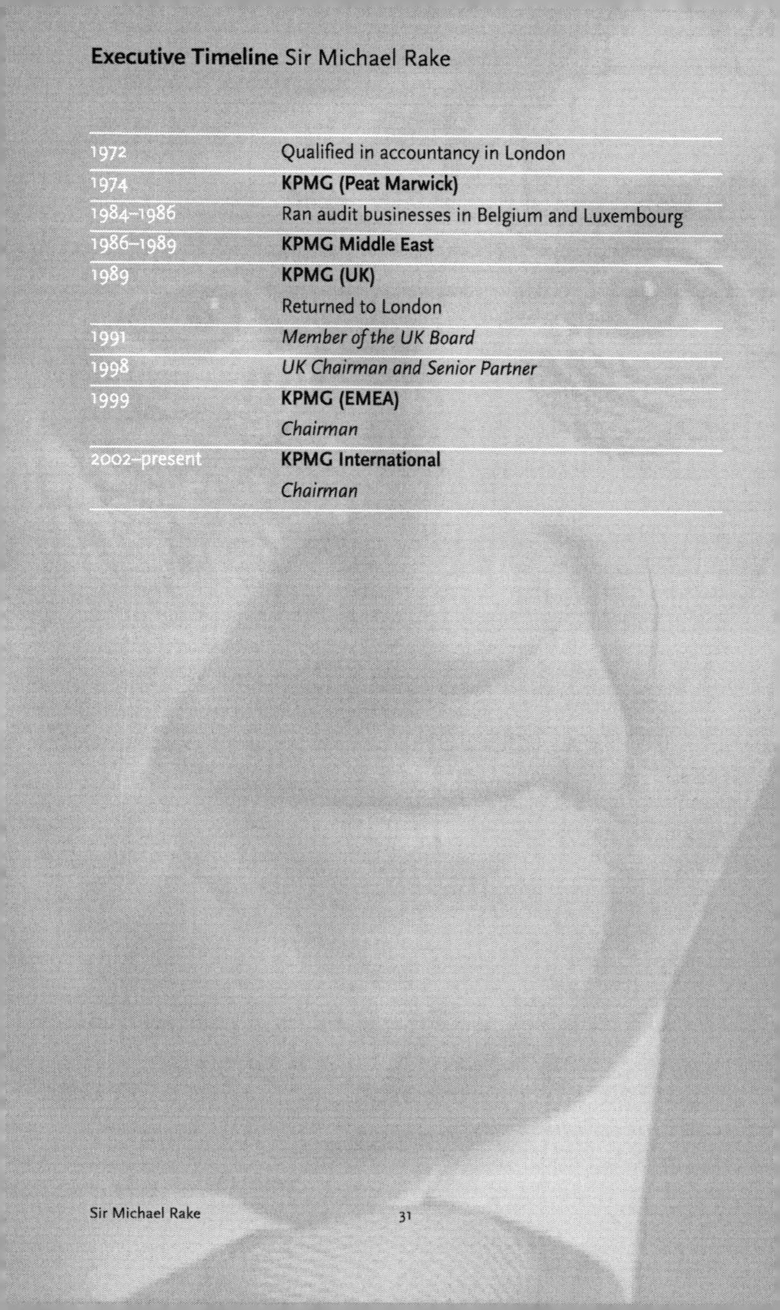

Executive Timeline Sir Michael Rake

1972	Qualified in accountancy in London
1974	**KPMG (Peat Marwick)**
1984–1986	Ran audit businesses in Belgium and Luxembourg
1986–1989	**KPMG Middle East**
1989	**KPMG (UK)** Returned to London
1991	*Member of the UK Board*
1998	*UK Chairman and Senior Partner*
1999	**KPMG (EMEA)** *Chairman*
2002–present	**KPMG International** *Chairman*

Companies must respond to competition and change by deciding how best to use their resources to achieve their overall goals. Chief Executives lead the process by setting a clear, achievable strategy that the management team must then execute.

3a Setting Clear and Achievable Goals

Roger Parry

Former Chairman and Chief Executive Officer, *Clear Channel International*

“My business career did not begin in business at all. I was a journalist for quite a long time, working for BBC and Independent Television, covering a whole range of topics, but towards the end of my journalistic career I was focusing on business issues. As a result, I was noticed by McKinsey & Company, the consulting firm. They recruited both myself and a business journalist from the *Financial Times* to join them as consultants. It was a real transition for me as I moved from being someone who made my living out of writing and broadcasting to someone who made my living out of problem solving, because consulting is all about problem solving.

I found that, having got a taste for business via the consulting environment, I wanted very quickly to move into business in a practical way. That's when I went into advertising with a company called WCRS. It then turned into another advertising business called Aegis, which was all about media buying. I have been quite fortunate along the way to have had some entrepreneurial roles: buying and selling a radio station; getting involved in buying into another advertising business, which I then sold on to an American media group. And that's how I ended up where I am now – running Clear Channel. I also hold non-executive roles as Chairman of a newspaper company, and Chairman of a magazine group. It is an extremely satisfying experience to sit as a Non-executive Chairman because you can observe the activities of a Chief Executive without having to carry their responsibilities.

Roger Parry

Former Chairman and Chief Executive Officer, *Clear Channel International*

Roger Parry left Clear Channel International in 2005. He is currently Chairman of Johnston Press.

To make decisions about future direction a Chief Executive needs to have a really thorough understanding of the issues facing the business, and of the environment within which it's operating.

When a Chief Executive sets goals he is really asking questions and making decisions about forward strategy before letting the management tier know what's expected of them. To make decisions about future direction a Chief Executive needs to have a really thorough understanding of the issues facing the business, and of the environment within which it's operating. Only as a consequence of having an understanding of that business environment can a Chief Executive set meaningful goals.

For example, if you have, as I do, a business that operates in more than fifty countries, it doesn't necessarily follow that each General Manager will share exactly the same goal. In China there is an enormous opportunity for growth, so the goal for the General Manager running our Chinese business unit is to look for new investments and ways of putting money to work. At the other end of the extreme is Switzerland, where the market is completely mature. The goal for the General Manager there is to operate at optimum efficiency; he is looking to do the same amount of business in a more effective way, whereas his Chinese counterpart is simply looking to do more business.

Another important consideration is 'do-ability' – a word that I don't think appears in any English dictionary. By that I mean: 'Is a goal actually achievable?' One of the worst things a CEO can say to an Operating Manager is: 'Here is your goal,' if the Operating Manager's response is: 'Such a thing is impossible.' We are all familiar with how that feels. If you say to a child: 'I want you to jump over a 10-metre hurdle,' the child knows that he can't do it, and will become very upset. In the same way, if you set business goals that are wholly unachievable, the net result will be very disappointed managers and a general feeling of failure.

Some years ago I was working within an advertising agency group where I was responsible for one of the public relations businesses that we had recently acquired. The Chief Executive told us that he wanted this business to double its sales within two years. Now the problem with aiming to double your sales within two years in a business like that is that you have to hire people to do the work. The constraint in this case wasn't winning new clients; the constraint was hiring people because at the time there was a great shortage of them. We walked away from that annual budget review knowing in advance that we were going to fail because it wasn't going to be possible to hire a sufficient number of people, or hire them quickly enough. The same goal – 'double your sales' – had been set for all the businesses across the whole group. We were stuck with something we couldn't possibly achieve and within a short period of time a lot of people were working with a sense of failure. The error was in the original process of setting the goal; everyone had to admit to that, and everyone had to be realistic about it.

When things go wrong it is important to review the problem, otherwise members of staff will become disaffected and the whole organization will become dysfunctional. It is very important that people have goals that are achievable so that they work with a sense of success. That does not mean setting goals that are so easy that everyone achieves them; it is not like following an examination process where everybody passes. The important thing is that if a goal is missed, it is missed for reasons that everyone understands and that can genuinely be put down to force majeure. A goal should not be missed because it was so unrealistic that it couldn't be achieved.

Clear goals are established as a result of really understanding the environment within which the business is operating, and also as a result of constructive dialogue between Business Managers and the Chief Executive. Appropriate goals are goals that all parties understand and buy into, rather than being unrealistic figures that are geared to impress shareholders.

It is a Chief Executive's responsibility to make sure that mergers and acquisitions really work. They must know how to get transactions done effectively, how to manage the integration process afterwards, and how to communicate this to stakeholders – both internally and externally.

Success or failure of an acquisition or a merger has to be down to the Chief Executive.

There's a real danger from a Chief Executive's point of view that during merger and acquisition transactions, the deal becomes the objective in itself, and people forget about what happens next, after the deal is done. The conventional wisdom is that success has been achieved when the champagne corks pop in the investment bank meeting room, when of course it hasn't. All you've actually done at that stage is bought something or merged with something. The challenge then is to make that acquisition or merger work. This is a responsibility that it's impossible for a Chief Executive to wriggle out of. If you are running a large business, you can sometimes say with legitimacy that you've devolved a lot of the responsibility to the Business Unit Managers and that success or failure within a business unit is down to them, but success or failure of an acquisition or a merger has to be down to the Chief Executive. That CEO is likely to have been the architect of that deal and should be deeply immersed in the issues relating to the transaction.

The first 100 days after the deal is done are the period during which the total focus should be upon making sure that the objectives of the merger or acquisition are clear and achievable. It's at that stage of a corporate marriage or acquisition that people are most confused, worried and in need of very clear direction. I've witnessed on a number of occasions the terrible sense of confusion that occurs during the first two or three months. There can be confusion regarding who is in charge and what the politics are, and there is a sense that in the higher echelons of management people are circling each other, jostling for position. It's an extremely damaging and debilitating period in the life of a business, and it is the role of the Chief Executive to stop the confusion. The answer is to take very early, very quick decisions regarding who is in charge, and if an office is to be closed, it should be announced quickly and closed down quickly to remove the uncertainty.

The issue of managing the transaction itself is easy. There are hundreds of investment bankers and lawyers who will manage the transaction for you, but the moment the deal is done they will vanish; they've all gone and you're left with the results. That's when a good Chief Executive comes into his or her own.

To make a merger or an acquisition successful you have to get as many people as you possibly can to buy into the logic of why the deal has been done in the first place. You have to communicate – you have to over-communicate – to make sure that people really understand what it's all about. It is the role of the Chief Executive at that point to become both visible and voluble in order to sell to everybody the reason a particular deal is being done. If you simply put out a five-line memo that says: 'We've done this deal,' you are not going to bring many people with you. You need to explain that the deal has been done because it will improve the product or it will make the service better or it will make the working conditions better. Emphasize the positives, explain why it has happened and make sure you tell everybody. There is an awful lot of communication required. It is a time when a Chief Executive should be highly visible, very active, and should be talking, writing notes and so on.

In a period of more steady growth Chief Executives should be more distant, but just after a merger or acquisition they need to champion their success, and go out and sell it to all the staff of both companies. It's a mistake to assume that because company A buys company B, the people in company A are not destabilized. In reality a good deal combines two businesses, so the people in the originating business may feel just as threatened as the people in the business that has been bought. The Chief Executive needs to sit down with all the managers from both businesses, the two that were merged or the two involved in the acquisition, to listen to them and understand their objectives. However, you can't spend too much time on it; you've got to do it in weeks rather than months. Then you need to tell them that you want them to create a single unified entity. That is the difficult bit because there will inevitably be conflict, and most of us don't really like that.

You are bound to have a situation where two people are doing the same job, and at the end of the day you can keep only one of them. Don't just leave the situation to resolve itself because it never will. It is a very difficult and unpleasant thing to have to say to someone who may be perfectly talented and skilled: 'I'm sorry but there are two of you here and you're the one who is going to go,' but if you take the decision early on you will be doing everyone a favour.

Making the deal work depends on telling everyone why you think the deal is a good idea and communicating how the process is going bring the two organizations together. ”

Executive Timeline Roger Parry

Early career	*Journalist* Seven years working for BBC, commercial TV and radio.
	McKinsey & Company Three years with the international firm of management consultants.
	WCRS An advertising business.
	Aegis Group *Development Director* Aegis is a global media planning and buying company.
1992	Was part of the team that managed the successful restructuring and refinancing of Aegis.
1995–1998	**More Group** *Chief Executive* A UK media company acquired by Clear Channel in 1998.
June 1998–2005	**Clear Channel International** *Chief Executive* Responsible for Clear Channel's operations in Europe, Asia/Pacific and Africa. The company is a world leader in out-of-home media.
2001–present	**Johnston Press** *Non-executive Chairman* A UK regional newspaper group.

To encourage your people to achieve the unexpected you need to give them room to breathe and the encouragement to drive and persevere – regardless of perceived odds and hurdles. By being given this chance to grow they can achieve some extraordinary things.

4 Persevere and Achieve the Unexpected

Amelia Fawcett

Director, *State Street Corporation*;
Former Vice Chairman and Chief Operating Officer, *Morgan Stanley International*

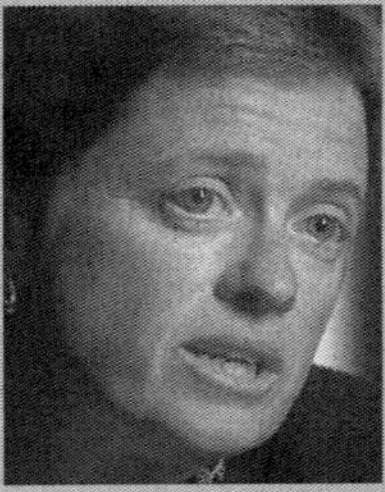

My Career

“I have had an interesting career and one that is not particularly traditional for an investment banker. After university I worked in New York as a paralegal because I had always wanted to be a lawyer – and, indeed, I did become a lawyer. I went to law school at the University of Virginia, and upon graduation moved to New York in the early 1980s to work at a major New York firm, Sullivan & Cromwell. There I focused mainly on banking, mergers and acquisitions and underwriting work. It was a very interesting time to be in New York – the beginning of the era of large international deals, large mergers and acquisitions transactions, and the growth of the financial services business generally.

Towards the end of 1985, Sullivan & Cromwell asked me to go and work in the firm's Paris office. I was very 'disappointed', since I really wanted to live and work in London. However, I was told that, since I spoke French, I was going to go to Paris. After the vibrancy and fast pace of New York, it was a very different place to be – there was not much going on in Financial Services, little public mergers and acquisitions work (much less 'hostile' deals) and the financial markets were rather sleepy – so very different from the Paris financial markets of today! I wondered what I was doing there, but in the end it was a great experience because I did so many different things.

I moved to Morgan Stanley in early 1987 to help set up a Legal and Compliance department. In the early days I focused very much on investment banking, mergers and acquisitions. I advised on the legal and operational sides of deals but gradually began doing more work on the sales and trading side (including derivatives and commodities), as well as being part of the team that opened offices in many countries. I think I have worked (in some capacity) on the opening or establishment of almost every Morgan Stanley office outside the United States, with the exception of Tokyo and Hong Kong. The experience allowed me to work with a variety of people who were building new businesses and looking for people who could help them 'execute' on business plans. So I was asked to come out of the legal department and work for the joint CEOs.

My Europe-wide remit was to work on 1) helping build businesses with governments, as well as policy initiatives with governments, 2) developing a media and communications strategy, and 3) developing community/CSR strategy led by senior management and 4) – as the firm really began to focus on strategic initiatives – to set up a strategy function, then an operational risk function.

I became Chief Administrative Officer and Managing Director in 1996 and Vice Chairman of Morgan Stanley in 2002. In addition I have done a lot of work, which I very much enjoy, outside the firm. Until recently, I was Deputy Chairman of the National Employment Panel. Now I am a member of the Court of the Bank of England, a trustee of the National Portrait Gallery, the Chairman of the London International Festival Theatre, a member of the Governing Council of the University of London and a Trustee of the National Maritime Museum (Cornwall), to name a few.

Amelia Fawcett

Director, *State Street Corporation*; former Vice Chairman and Chief Operating Officer, *Morgan Stanley*

Amelia Fawcett left her position as Vice Chairman and Chief Operating Officer in September 2006. She is currently a Director for State Street Corporation.

Persevere and Achieve the Unexpected

I have been impressed over a very long time, both from personal experience and from business experience, at how important perseverance is in achieving the unexpected. I suppose it goes back to being a small child. My grandfather's sister, Aunt Rebecca, used to say to me when I had been particularly difficult: 'Amelia, remember to put your best foot forward...' and I would think: 'Yeah, yeah, yeah...I've heard that before,' but then would come the 'kicker' as she said sternly: 'and keep it there!' That concept of constantly striving and persevering is a lesson well learned as a child. I'd use it even in fishing. You look for a fish and you can't find it or you lose it after presenting a perfect fly to it and then you fish the river for the rest of the day. But in the back of your mind is the recurring thought: 'No, dammit, I'm not going to lose that fish...' So you go back, with a different approach and a different fly, and, sure enough, you land the largest fish of the day.

More recently, the importance of this approach became very clear to me at Morgan Stanley – a large, international financial services firm where technology and systems are global. The perceived wisdom always had been that for a firm to be efficient, solutions had to be global, but global solutions can be time-consuming. In an era when we really needed to be more innovative and cost-effective, it seemed odd to me that we couldn't find a way, on a regional basis, to make the business more effective and efficient, even if it was part of a global whole. I wasn't willing to take the view that there was nothing we could do in Europe to improve and, in doing

‘Put your best foot forward…and keep it there.’

so, help the global business overall. With all the talented individuals we had, we should have been able to find a solution to take the business – and particularly the operational side of the business – to a different level.

I brought together the top forty people from the infrastructure side of the business. They had varying expertise and were from varying backgrounds: everything from finance to operations to technology. I took them off site (away from the office) and divided them into four groups of ten. I gave each group two days to come up with a business plan for a new business that they would put to venture capitalists (i.e., me and a few other senior managers) to bid for $50 million of investment.

Interestingly, at the end of the two days, every single group came back with the same operational matrix; namely, in order to get a business started and keep it efficient and cost-effective, they would use alternative sourcing, joint ventures or outsourcing. That begged the question for me, and I think for the whole group: ‘Why don't we do this back at the office? What's different here?’ I then pushed for a group of senior managers to take time away from their day jobs, over a period of several weeks, to analyse all the businesses, all the processes in Europe (line by line), with a view to finding out whether there was a way we could change the paradigm and our working model.

Sure enough, at the end of the process, they came back with a variety of proposals, including a strategy that had been mooted in one of the off-site business proposals. The proposal was to undertake a fair amount of our processing and technology in a different, more cost-effective environment (which in this case, after a detailed search, was determined to be Scotland). In the end, all the time committed by this dedicated group of people had been more than cost-effective: while the initial operation in Scotland required upfront investment, after a relatively short period of time they had covered all the cost of that investment. Now their recommendations are continuing to return a serious amount of money to the firm. That's a significant benefit.

But there are other things that we've learnt as well. First, other parts of the firm decided that they could benefit from the same operating model, so the model of alternative sourcing has popped up in Australia and in the United States. Second, we instigated a way of thinking about our business and an enthusiasm in a group of people who didn't think they had the leeway to go ahead and make a difference. Their excitement about striving to change the business was almost as valuable as the actual net savings the firm has achieved over the same period of time.

It was a great revelation to all of us that, despite being told that a solution couldn't be found, we stuck with it, we got the right people in the room, we encouraged them to focus on the right things, we gave them the latitude to make some interesting choices, and we allowed them to go ahead and run with the strategy. The benefits have been positive both for the company and the individuals involved, as demonstrated by the way in which they have developed as a very strong group of managers.

When you take time to encourage and inspire a group of people to think outside the box, to be creative, and you give them the room to grow, they do just that. People can achieve extraordinary things, but it does take some courage on their part, and on the part of senior management. It also takes a fair amount of commitment in terms of time to encourage them and to allow them the freedom to push the boundaries, but in doing so they grow, because they know that they did it themselves.

What I learned, and I think we all learned as a result, is: 'Never say die.' And if I come back to my Aunt Rebecca, it really is about 'putting your best foot forward and keeping it there'. Whether you're fishing or whether you're growing your business, the areas of focus, commitment, determination and follow-through – which this extraordinary group of individuals showed clearly over a period of time – are essential. They are essential in your personal life, and they are essential in your business life. I think our team now does put its best foot forward and keeps it there. ”

Executive Timeline Amelia Fawcett

1974–1978	Degree in history, Wellesley College, USA.
1978–1980	**Sullivan & Cromwell** *Paralegal* Major New York law firm
1980–1983	University of Virginia School of Law (JD)
1983–1986	**Sullivan & Cromwell** *Lawyer* Worked in New York and Paris.
1987	**Morgan Stanley** Joined the London office of this large, international financial services firm. She has since been with the firm, and in London, for more than 18 years.
1990	*Vice President*
1992	*Executive Director*
1996	*Managing Director and Chief Administrative Officer* for the European operations
2002–2006	**Morgan Stanley International** *Vice Chairman and Chief Operating Officer*
2006–present	**State Street Corporation** *Director*

The toughest decisions you make are the ones where you reach out to the people whose opinion, position and input are most important to you, and half of them tell you to go north and half of them tell you to go south

5 Make The Tough Call, Then Act

David Brandon

Chairman and Chief Executive Officer, *Domino's Pizza*

"I was born and raised in the great State of Michigan. I went to the University of Michigan on a football scholarship. I was a four-year athlete and I graduated from the University of Michigan with a degree in speech communications. I was recruited to go to work for Proctor & Gamble. I worked there for about five years in their sales and sales management programme, and at the end of a great training experience and a wonderful management experience as a very young businessperson, I was afforded the ability to join a very small start-up company that had a great product idea and one that I believed in. I was there for 20 years.

Valassis was the name of the company. We began as a company with about $30 million in sales, a few dozen employees, publishing printed sales promotion materials to branded marketers. By the time I left there, 20 years later, we were a New York Stock Exchange listed company with about a $2 billion market cap, we had about 1,450 employees, about $800 million in sales and we had been named one of the hundred best companies to work for in America for three consecutive years. I was very proud of the way we built that culture, we built that company, we created tremendous value for our shareholders.

And for the last six and a half years of my career I have been proud to be the Chairman and CEO of Domino's Pizza. Domino's Pizza is a global brand. We have nearly 8,000 stores in 55 countries around the world. We employ about

150,000 people across that system and we're in the business of providing delivered pizza to folks all over the world in a very convenient, safe and great-tasting manner.

David Brandon

Chairman and Chief Executive Officer, *Domino's Pizza*

For 20 years prior to coming to Domino's, I ran a great organization called Valassis. We were in the publishing business and had a number of products. There was one very critical time fairly early on in the stage of our development where a well-financed and very legitimate competitor came into our industry. They announced a product innovation that was totally different to what we had been doing with our core business.

So, we were in a situation where this new player on the block came in with something very exciting, innovative and new. It was very different to what we had built our core business around in terms of concept and execution. I remember it as one of the first times in my career where I was confronted with one of those strategic decisions that could truly be one of those 'bet the company' situations. If you get it right there's going to be great rewards, but if you get it wrong the consequences could be absolutely devastating. I remember that it was one of the first major decisions where, as a leader, I found myself in a situation where there were two camps. It was almost a 50/50 vote, because all leaders reach out and try to get consensus.

The learning that I got from that experience – and I've remembered this and played it through in my head many, many times as I've made decisions over the years – was that when you go into a room with a bunch of really smart people that you hired, that you trust, and that you work with every day, and a problem gets put on the table to which there's 100 per cent consensus as to what the course of action should be, that's the easiest decision you'll make as a leader. There's just no problem making the right decision, because there's total consensus.

There have also been a few times where I've gotten off the page, and the problem will be put on the table and 100 per cent of the people who work for me say: 'Dave, I don't think we want to go down that road.' For me, that's a relatively easy decision too, because I can't think of too many times where 100 per cent of my team says to go north and my desire is to try to go south.

I think if that were ever to happen as a leader you should question whether you've really got the right team, if you think they're all that wrong. So, that's a pretty easy decision. The toughest decisions you make are the ones where you reach out to the people whose opinion, position and input are most important to you, and half of them tell you to go north and half of them tell you to go south. That was the situation that I encountered in this particular circumstance many years ago.

Here's what I learnt from that experience: it's the hardest decision a leader has to make. And what we all have to understand as leaders in business when we're confronted with that dynamic is that leaders must lead. That is the magic moment where a leader has got to step forward and say:

Organizations look to their leaders for leadership, and what they want to see is confidence, passion and a true sense of calm

'Here's the direction we're taking.' The approach that you take to making that decision is important; but what you do after you make that decision is almost more important.

If you can stand before your organization with passion, conviction and perseverance and say: 'Here's where we're going, here's why, and here's why it's important that we all rally around this decision – even those of you who would have made a different decision', the way that you can mobilize and energize your organization to embrace that decision and go out and execute against it is huge.

In that particular case, it turned out that I clearly made the right decision, but I'll never know for sure whether the decision was as important as the way the decision was implemented. I remember from my days as an athlete that when you looked over on the bench and the coach looked confident and under control, and had a look on their face that basically said: 'I know we're going to win despite this tough situation', as a player you performed better. Organizations look to their leaders for leadership, and what they want to see is confidence, passion and a true sense of calm that 'I've made the right choice; let's go run the play and let's win.'

The postscript to the story was that the competitor who came into the business continued to try to be the innovator and create excitement around a brand new concept, and we became the tried and true proven performer in the category. Over time the newness of their concept wore off and people basically said: 'You know, there's reasons why this Valassis company has been successful and grown to the point that they have; the fundamental core product that they have performs best the way it is.' It was only a couple of years later that we acquired the other company, as a result of its being in a very weakened position that could no longer compete.

So, our organization lived through the whole process: the tough decision, executing and defending our position, weakening our opponent or our competitor, and then ultimately celebrated the day that we bought what was left of the other business, incorporated it into our company and that made us even larger and more dominant. ”

The magic moment where a leader has got to step forward and say: 'Here's the direction we're taking.'

Executive Timeline David Brandon

Early years	**Procter & Gamble** *Sales Management*
1979–1989	**Valassis Inc.** A company in the sales promotion and coupon industries that went public during his tenure.
1989–1998	*President and Chief Executive Officer*
1996–1998	*Chairman*
1999–present	**Domino's Pizza** *Chairman and Chief Executive Officer* International restaurant business (Ann Arbor, Michigan).
2001–present	**The TJX Companies, Inc.** *Director* Off-price apparel and home fashions retailer.
2003–present	**Burger King Corporation** *Director* International restaurant business (Miami, Florida).
2004–present	**Kaydon Corp.** *Director* Specialty engineering and manufacturing (Ann Arbor, Michigan).

The informal interactions are as important – and I would argue even more important – in leadership than the formal, structured, canned interactions that happen so often day in and day out in our business lives. That informal interaction is how somebody will form their opinion of you.

6 Leadership 24/7

Ken Freeman

Managing Director, *KKR*

"I always wanted to be a musician, at least from the age of five. I went off to college and soon discovered that I wanted to eat more than I wanted to play music. I went to Bucknell University in central Pennsylvania, ended up getting a degree in business, but it had more music than business to it in those days, in the early 70s.

I was able to get a job in finance at a company called Corning Glass, as an internal auditor with one accounting course to my name, no intention to become a CPA, but a deep desire to eat. That story of starting to work for Corning in Internal Audit, led to a career at Corning of over 25 years. I started in Internal Audit, was a financial person for 15 years, was the Corporate Controller of Corning in the late 1980s, a time when Corning was going through its dramatic change period of restructuring the company and selling or shutting down over one-third of its assets around the world. And at the end of the 1980s – 1989, I went from being a guy that was counting the money, to becoming a guy that was trying to make the money. Corning asked me to go run one of its businesses.

It was a deep turnaround. It was a science glass and plastics business for research labs. A small business for Corning, 75 years old, that had long been neglected and had long been marginally, at best, profitable, began the turnaround of the science business. And then I went off to run Corning Asahi Video Products, a television glass-making business for Corning that had been invented by Corning many, many decades earlier and had been unprofitable for almost two decades itself, when I arrived. We executed a dramatic turnaround in that business and grew the business.

And then I was asked to go back to the Headquarters of Corning and, and run all the staff groups at Corning except for the scientists and the lawyers and the treasurers. Everybody else from communications to control to HR was under my jurisdiction at that time, and I ran a large restructuring and re-engineering project for Corning at that time, and we were building capabilities for growth. At the same time we were reducing significant levels of costs from around the company.

In May of '95 I joined Quest Diagnostics, then known as Corning Clinical Labs, ostensibly for a one-year hitch. It turned out to be a 10-year hitch as the business was in need of a significant turnaround. We were spun off entirely by Corning at the end of 1996, a year and a half after my arrival, and from that time onward I was Chairman and CEO, until the end of 2004 – about nine and a half years – a period where we turned the company around, saved it, built the company, took decisive industry leadership by buying the biggest company in the industry, continued to grow the business through acquisition as well as through organic growth through scientific methods, gene-based testing, and created a dramatic amount of value, fortunately, for our shareholders.

When we were all said and done, we took a company from about $1.5 billion in revenues at the beginning to over

$5 billion in revenues, about 14,000 employees to over 37,000, and, and market capitalization on the street of about $350 million in the beginning to over $9 billion on the date of my retirement from the company at the end of 2004. Today, I'm managing director at Kohlberg Kravis Roberts, a large private equity firm in New York City, focused on healthcare and industrial investments. I'm also spending time at Columbia Business Schools and enjoying my family – two children who are grown adults now and my wife of over 32 years.

Ken Freeman

Managing Director, *KKR*

Even when we think a chance meeting with somebody might not have any value, the end result is that every moment of every day our leadership shines through, good or bad.

I'd been running Quest Diagnostics for about two or three years, and we were in the middle of our turnaround. We'd gone through stopping the bleeding and stabilizing the business, and were starting to see, ever so slightly, some gradual improvement. I was on the first vacation I'd taken in eons with my wife, our daughter and our son. We had gone to Orlando to spend some time in central Florida for a spring break, and we were heading to the airport. We got to the airport a little bit early, went through the security gates, and were walking towards the specific gate for our flight back to the New York area.

All of a sudden, an individual came running up to me, and said: 'You're Ken Freeman.' Now, you can imagine my 15-year-old daughter and my 12-year-old son were rather inspired by this: 'Gee dad; here's somebody in the middle of Orlando airport coming up to you and saying "you're Ken Freeman"'. I girded myself and replied: 'Yes; yes I am.' And as the discussion moved on he said: 'I want to introduce myself. You met me about a month ago here in Florida.' I had been over in Tampa then at one of the big labs we have. He continued:

'I'm a courier for Quest Diagnostics. I just want you to know, Ken, that I've met you once and I've attended a town meeting personally, and I come to the virtual town meetings where we see you and hear from you and listen to your voice mails. And I just wanted you to know that I am in your corner. We are going to turn this company around; we're going to become a great company; your leadership is going to get us there, and I'm going to be one of those folks on the ground that's going to make it happen. And Ken, I'd like you to meet my family.'

I introduced my family to his family, we became fast friends, we chatted for five or ten minutes, and in the end we parted good friends; and, even more importantly, I think my kids were inspired. They asked: 'Gee dad, is this how business really works?' And I answered: 'Well, kids, it can work a lot of different ways; but there's a lesson from this chance encounter in the middle of nowhere. I could have reacted to this guy and said: "Who are you? I don't want to talk to you, I'm here with my family; I'm on vacation and I don't want to be upset with my family in an airport", as opposed to being nice to an employee and engaging him in a constructive way. What do we see?' And my family replied: 'Well, gee, what we saw was an interaction of two people who really seemed to get along.' I said: 'That's the issue.'

The lesson of leadership here is really very simple: as leaders and as individuals we have to be who we are 24 hours a day, seven days a week. The informal interactions are as important

– and I would argue even more important – in leadership than the formal, structured, canned interactions that happen so often day in and day out in our business lives. That informal interaction is how somebody will form their opinion of you.

People want their leaders to be human beings above all else. They hear so many of us talk about values and behaviours, and what it takes to make our company strong, and if we don't exhibit those behaviours in those informal settings – for example if I'd been yelling at my family or even having an altercation of some sort, like so often happens in airports all over this country – how would that employee have reacted? He would say: 'Well, he doesn't walk the talk of the values he keeps talking about.'

The most exciting part of a situation like the Orlando incident is that the courier didn't keep quiet about it. He went back and told his colleagues in the Tampa laboratory: 'I met Ken and his family at the airport. They're all nice people and they really are committed to helping us turn our company around. I told him I'm committed too, and we can't let Ken down; we can't let our business down.' And it spread to the couriers department; it spread beyond that into the overall laboratory in Tampa, Florida. So, even when we think a chance meeting with somebody might not have any value, the end result is that every moment of every day our leadership shines through, good or bad. And whatever shines through, good or bad, is going to get communicated beyond the little circle where the actual dialogue took place. ”

Executive Timeline Ken Freeman

1972–1985	**Corning, Inc.** *Internal Auditor* Manufacturer of specialty glass and ceramics
1985–1987	*Vice President and Corporate Controller*
1987–1989	*Senior Vice President*
1989–1990	*General Manager* of the Science Products Division
1990–1993	**Corning Asahi Video Products** *CEO*
1993–1995	*Executive Vice President*
1995–1996	**Corning Clinical Laboratories** *President and CEO*
1996	Corning spins off healthcare services company into **Quest Diagnostics**
1996–2004	**Quest Diagnostics** *Chairman, President, and CEO* Led an increase in market capitalization from $350 million to more than $9 billion
2005–present	**KKR (Kohlberg Kravis Roberts & Co)** *Managing Director* Private equity firm

Being a visible leader is important – especially in a multinational organization. A closed-door policy never works because the leader will be cut off from the organization. It is vital to make time for daily, face-to-face communication with your staff. A leader who is never seen will not be recognized.

7 Visible Leadership

Sir Richard Evans

Chairman, *United Utilities*

"I have spent most of my working life in the aerospace business, but I came into it from a humble beginning. When I was starting out I never thought that I had received any guidance in the shaping and development of my career. Having become a bit smarter later on, I came to realize that there is a degree of organization within companies that tends to single people out and monitor their performance to see whether they have what it takes to move into more senior positions. Most of the moves I've made, particularly in the early stages of senior management, came as big surprises to me; they were not appointments that I'd ever imagined I would take at the time that I took them.

The really big move came when I was made Chief Executive of British Aerospace. I think it's fair to say that had I known at the time what I was walking into, I might have thought somewhat longer and harder about whether I should take the job. It was a seriously difficult assignment, with an immense number of problems that I didn't understand when I took on the role. Indeed, I don't think the company really understood quite what the issues were.

I spent longer in the Chief Executive's slot inside British Aerospace and then BAE Systems than I'd ever expected to. At that time the natural progression would have been for the Chief Executive to move on, and to take up a Chairmanship. I had never intended to become Chairman of British Aerospace; I took on the role on account of a set of domestic situations that arose for the then Chairman, Bob Bowman. Bob was an American, and he had to leave the UK to go back to the States. We didn't have time to undertake the usual search and selection process, so I came into the Chairmanship not as a part of conscious succession planning, but as an emergency interim appointment. A similar situation applied at United Utilities. I had been a Non-executive Director at United Utilities for a relatively short period of time when, tragically, the then Chairman of the company died very suddenly. My home was, and still is, in the northwest of England, where United Utilities is based. After first testing the market, the Board asked me if I would step up from my Non-executive position to become Chairman of the company.

I finished up at the top of two FTSE 100 companies via a set of circumstances that were complete chance. I had originally anticipated that, having finished my term as Chief Executive in British Aerospace, I would be able to regain control of my life and spend more time with my wife and family. That's still what I'm trying to achieve, but it's not proving to be as easy as I had expected.

Sir Richard Evans

Chairman, *United Utilities*

It's important to me that people see the leader around the organization. If you're controlling a vast multinational, you should be seen around it as often as possible.

I'm a great believer in visibility in leadership. It's important to me that people see the leader around the organization. If you're controlling a vast multinational, you should be seen around it as often as possible. Simple physical limitations will restrict the amount of time that can be spent in different parts of the building, but when I walk in to my office in the morning, I like people to see me arrive, I like to say hello to people and ask them what they have they been doing at the weekend so that they know I'm there. I like them to see that I'm working reasonably hard on their and the shareholders' behalf, and providing the sort of leadership that they will want to follow.

I dislike any form of leadership that closes itself off behind an office door. I've always operated a very clear policy of never shutting my office door, unless there's a fairly big meeting taking place. If it's a small meeting, rarely do I close the office door. That conveys a message. I have an aversion to working in buildings where everybody is sitting in individual offices: those are places where people hide. They go in there to keep

Invariably, as you progressed through the organization, you ended up with an office on the 'Golden Mile'. Managers had made it to the top of the organization, but could barely see from one end of the corridor to the other.

out of the way and out of sight: such action speaks volumes about the quality of a person in leadership terms.

In my early days in senior management we were housed in a grandiose, purpose-built building in outer London. There were two wonderful long corridors in this building: one was appropriately entitled the 'Silver Mile', and the other the 'Golden Mile'. Invariably, as you progressed through the organization, you ended up with an office on the 'Golden Mile'. Managers had made it to the top of the organization, but could barely see from one end of the corridor to the other. No one ever saw another person walking along it. The first time I was located there to work I suggested that we should pipe in some organ music because it was like walking into a funeral parlour. Everybody had a wonderful office, but there were no open doors. You never saw a warm body while you were in the building, and it was the most soulless place imaginable. The working people never saw the management or the leadership of the business. Now that is utterly horrendous. My instinct was just to rip the walls down – until it was explained to me that the building would collapse if we did so. Others said it could cost too much to relocate to another building to work in. What complete rubbish! In fact, money would be saved because, provided management visibility improved, performance would improve.

If you want to make leadership work, first of all the leader has to be visible. A leader who is never seen will not be recognized as a leader.

If you want to make leadership work, first of all the leader has to be visible. A leader who is never seen will not be recognized as a leader. To be a visible leader takes work, and you've got to make time for it. You've got an office to run, you've got to keep the in-tray moving, you've got to take the telephone calls – but you've also got to make time to get around and go around. If it's a large organization, the leader needs to be prepared to do a lot of travelling.

Anybody who wants to sit inside a closed office along a passageway is not for me. If you want people to follow you, they've got to be able to see you and they've got to be

To be a visible leader takes work, and you've got to make time for it.

able to talk to you. If that is not your style, then get out of management and go and do something else. ”

Executive Timeline Sir Richard Evans

1960	**Ministry of Transport and Civil Aviation**
1967	**Ferranti** *Government Contracts Officer* Ferranti was a global organization known for technological innovation. It closed in 1994 after one hundred years of trading.
1969	**British Aircraft Corporation** Joined the Military Aircraft Division.
1978	*Commercial Director* – Warton Division, British Aerospace (BAe)
1981	*Assistant Managing Director* – Warton Division
1983–1986	*Deputy Managing Director* Appointed following BAe Aircraft Group managerial changes.
1986	*Deputy Managing Director (and Managing Director Designate)* – British Aerospace Military Aircraft Division
1987	*Marketing Director – British Aerospace* Appointed to the Board.
1988	*Chairman* – British Aerospace Defence companies
1990	*Chief Executive* – British Aerospace
1996	Knighted in the 1996 Queen's Birthday Honours.
1997	**United Utilities** Joined the Board as a Non-executive Director. United Utilities manages water and wastewater networks in Wales and wastewater treatment facilities in Scotland.
1998–2004	*Chairman* – British Aerospace Continued to chair the company when it became BAE Systems following the merger with Marconi Electronic Systems. Retired from this position in July 2004, but continue to support the company in an advisory capacity.
2001–present	**United Utilities** *Chairman*

The key point that I really got out of that experience was that you are a role model 100 per cent of the time. When you're CEO of a company, you can't separate your personal life from your professional life. People learn what you do in your personal life.

8 Matching Your Actions to Your Words

Paul Anderson

Chairman, *Spectra Energy*

"I got an engineering degree at the University of Washington, and then I found out what engineers did, and decided I really didn't do that very well, so I went on to business school at Stanford University and went to the Graduate School of Business there and got an MBA. Upon leaving Stanford, I joined Ford Motor Company, and I was a car designer for eight years, or a car planner, depending on how you know the industry.

And then at the end of eight years I, almost by mistake, ended up in the energy business in Houston for a company called Texas Eastern Transmission Company. I thought they actually manufactured transmissions. It was a bit of a misunderstanding when I started at the interview.

Then I stayed in the energy business really for the next 20 years, progressing through Texas Eastern; I went through a merger with Panhandle Eastern, at which point I took a year off to become Chief Financial Officer of Inland Steel in Chicago; came back to Panhandle Eastern who had acquired Texas Eastern, worked my way to the CEO of that company, and merged it with Duke Power to create Duke Energy.

At which point, again, I was without portfolio, so I left for Australia and spent the next few years as managing director of BHP, which ultimately became BHP Billiton. One of the last things I did was to merge those two companies together, and BHP Billiton is now the largest resources company in the world. At which point I retired, and thought that I was done with my business career, moved back to Maine and got a call from the Board of Duke Energy asking would I come and spend a few years sort of getting the ox out of the ditch with Duke Energy as their CEO and Chairman.

Paul Anderson

Chairman, *Spectra Energy*

Paul Anderson stepped down as Chairman of Duke Energy in 2007, and is now Chairman of Spectra Energy.

Once I had spent about a year at BHP Billiton, the company was really getting back on track and all the measures of success were pretty positive. Certainly profitability was up and our efficiency was up; we were getting great productivity and you could look at almost any measure and it was positive – except safety.

Safety had actually gone down a little bit. I was very vexed by this, and I kept asking the head of the safety group: 'What is it – how come the organization isn't embracing a safety culture, and how come we can't seem to improve our safety performance?'

After beating round the bush for a while, he finally blurted it out. He said: 'Well, you're the problem.' And I said: 'I'm the problem? I'm a real proponent of safety; we've got it right in our charter; I can't imagine a higher objective for the company; I can't imagine anything going before it.' And he said: 'Well, you're a lousy role model – just look at what you're doing.' I replied: 'Lousy role model – what do you mean?' He said: 'People notice that when you come to work you jaywalk across the street – you don't go to the corner. People notice that when you're out visiting a plant, if you're wearing dark safety glasses and you come inside, you take off the dark glasses even if you don't have a pair of clear safety glasses to replace them with and you're still in an area where you need them. They notice that when you go up and down steps you don't hold onto the handrail, which is the standard practice we have here. They notice that you don't park your car backwards into a parking space, which, again, is the safety standard that we have. You're just basically a lousy role model.'

Of course, that took me a little aback. But he went on and said: 'When you go to visit a manager, the first thing you say is "How're you doing against budget?" You start asking financial questions, you don't start with: "How is your safety programme? What results have you had over the last year? What are your two or three safety issues that you have here?" So, people assume you're not particularly interested in safety. And in fact, they're focusing on everything but safety because you really haven't highlighted it.'

That really struck me. I mean, I had not before been in a situation where I was so clearly scrutinized as a role model and where safety was so important, because this was primarily a mining operation and steel mills, and very much an industrial setting. I realised that not only was I being scrutinized on the job, I was being scrutinized off it too.

One of the things that the head of the safety group said was: 'People know you don't like to wear a helmet when you ride a motorcycle.' And I thought: 'Well, what's that got to do with anything?' But if you don't display these values in your personal life, then you obviously don't really embrace the values. It really drove home the point. Somebody once said: 'Good leadership is doing the right thing, even when no one's looking.' I realised that actually, somebody was looking. It wasn't the case that no one was looking.

So I really took that to heart, and there's a good ending to this story because once I realised how important it was to establish myself as a good role model I took it on as a personal passion to improve the safety programme there; to get personally involved, to set myself up as role model – and it really had an impact on the organization.

The fact that you are the role model has a huge impact on what the organization is going to do.

The stats got bigger, and it was very gratifying to me because when you have 50,000 people, a slight improvement in the stats is actually a huge reduction in human suffering in terms of what actually happens out there in the field. In fact, when I came to Duke Energy, the first thing I did was look at the safety programme and start talking safety, because I realised the impact that you have at the top, and the fact that you are the role model has a huge impact on what the organization is going to do.

The key point that I really got out of that experience was that you are a role model 100 per cent of the time. When you're

If you don't match your words with your actions, the organization basically discards your words.

CEO of a company, you can't separate your personal life from your professional life.

People learn what you do in your personal life; they follow what's going on; they watch you in situations where you might even think you're not being watched. And if you don't walk the talk, they pick that up in a heartbeat. They will sense very quickly whether your words and your actions are tied together, and if you don't match your words with your actions, the organization basically discards your words. ”

Executive Timeline Paul Anderson

Early years	**Ford Motor Company** Held various positions in marketing, product engineering, finance, and manufacturing.
1977	**PanEnergy** Held various leadership positions, including Chairman, President, and CEO. Provider of natural gas, with four major interstate transmission lines.
1997	Duke Power acquires PanEnergy
1997–1998	**Duke Energy** *President and Chief Operating Officer*
1998–2001	**BHP Limited** *Managing Director and CEO*
2001	BHP Limited merges with Billiton
2001–2002	**BHP Billiton Ltd (Australia)** **BHP Billiton plc (UK)** Retired as *Managing Director* and *CEO*
2003–2007	**Duke Energy** Leading energy company (Charlotte, North Carolina) *Chairman and CEO*
2007–present	**Spectra Energy** Duke Energy spins off its natural gas business into Spectra Energy *Chairman*
2002–present	**Qantas Airways** *Director*
2006–present	**BHP Billiton Ltd** and **BHP Billiton Plc** *Director*

All leaders, in all situations, have to make tough calls. Don't shy away from making those decisions; be ready to stand up and be counted. You don't need to win a popularity contest, so don't confuse being popular with the need to make the right choices.

9a Leadership is not a Popularity Contest

Sanjiv Ahuja

Chief Executive Officer, *Orange Group*

“I completed an undergraduate degree in electrical engineering and then went to the United States, where I did a Masters at Columbia University in New York. I went to work for IBM in 1979. I grew through the ranks and became a mid-level executive leading one of IBM's software businesses. I left IBM in 1994 to go to Bell Communications Research and was there until 2000. I left as the President of the company. I then moved into the venture capital business for a couple of years before I came to Orange. I've been the Chief Executive Officer of Orange since early 2004.

Sanjiv Ahuja

Chief Executive Officer, *Orange Group*

As a leader of a business, be very clear in your mind that you are not running a democracy; leaders must be prepared to exercise the authority that comes with a leadership role.

There is a big myth in business: that you need your team to buy into your strategy. There is another big myth: that leaders need to win a popularity contest inside their company. As a leader of a business, be very clear in your mind that you are not running a democracy; leaders must be prepared to exercize the authority that comes with a leadership role.

When you make decisions, when you make choices, they will not always be the most popular choices. If your objective is to ensure that your team buys into your strategy or likes what you do, then you are not needed as a leader. You could operate a continuous poll of ideas to determine what decision and what direction the company ought to move in; you could do that from morning to night. Everybody would work on it and the business would be rudderless.

As a leader you are supposed to make some decisions that aren't necessarily going to be very popular and that is okay; but stand up and be counted for those decisions. Sometimes decisions are needed that will put your job on the line; but that's okay too – stand up and be counted for those decisions.

When you look at the history of mankind, all successful leaders at different stages of their life have had to make those types of decisions. If these become 'bet your job' decisions, that's okay; people make 'bet your life' decisions every day. Most of the decisions we make are not that critical; but we must still make them and not be deluded by the absolute myth that it is necessary to be a popular leader. You need to be an *effective* leader, you need to be a *decisive* leader, but once you are leading with effectiveness, decisiveness, clarity and a passion for the success of your business, your team will follow you.

Sometimes decisions are needed that will put your job on the line; but that's okay – stand up and be counted for those decisions.

Around ten years ago I was brought into a business where employee morale was low, product quality was poor and profits were in a terrible shape. The revenue had been in decline for a number of years. Most of the customers doubted that the business could be turned around; a few of the employees thought that too. When I stepped in I had to make a significant number of changes. I changed most of the leadership team, I changed a good portion of the management team that worked for those leaders; essentially I restructured the business.

Once you are leading with effectiveness, decisiveness, clarity and a passion for the success of your business, your team will follow you.

In the early days I wasn't the most popular leader, but by the time we had completed the transformation the company was delivering world-class performance in terms of quality, delivery, productivity, profitability and growth. The company met all performance criteria in a world-class manner and I would like to say that by the time I left I was probably the most popular leader that company had ever had. Had I been looking for employee accolades, I probably would not have taken any of the tough decisions that I had to take.

All leaders, in all situations, have to make the tough calls. Don't shy away from making those calls; be ready to stand up and be counted. Don't confuse popularity with the need to make the right choices. Right choices and popularity do not have to go hand in hand.

A leader who is true to his or her personal values creates a personal 'brand' of leadership. Clear communication of leadership values provides people with decision-making criteria that are understood and encourage world-class performance.

A brand represents values: it means all the values associated with the product, service or person are obvious.

Just as all successful products and services are branded, so too it is essential that you as a leader have a brand. What does 'brand' mean? A brand represents values: it means all the values associated with the product, service or person are obvious. A brand should be consistent time after time, day in and day out, year after year, so that people are able to recognize what it is that this individual, this leader, in whatever endeavour they are engaged, stands for.

Leaders can be demanding; leaders can expect a lot from their team. Leaders can be hard working, they can be decisive or they can demonstrate innovation. Leaders can also sometimes be negative. Every individual, every leader in the history of mankind has stood for certain things. One of the first things that I did when I became CEO of Orange was to talk to my teams. I spoke to all the people who reported to me in all the different countries. I told each of the teams what I stood for. I told them what they could count on me for, day in and day out; I told them how I would react to situations when they talked to me. I laid it out, I was clear; I put it on the table.

Simultaneously, I laid out my expectations of them. I talked about world-class performance; I told them that I am very demanding, that I am passionate, that I stand for Orange values, that I would stand up for the team and that I deliver to my own expectations. Then I said I expect world-class performance from them in return: day in and day out. Having told them what I stand for, and what their expectations should be, I could then equally and clearly state my demands and set my expectations of the team, and expect that it would get done because I provided clarity.

> I told each of the teams what I stood for. I told them how I would react to situations when they talked to me.

Sometimes in business there are pressures to get a product to market before it is ready. Market pull is attempting to bring the product out sooner than it's ready, and there might even be an internal move to push the product out before the right time. As a leader, if you stand for quality, you have to step up and say: 'We will not ship the product before it's ready.' We take that stance within Orange.

Sometimes our focus on quality may mean that our product or service launches are delayed. We are not always first to the market. We were not first to the marketplace with 3G in either the UK or in France; we got it out when it was ready. We said we wouldn't ship it and we wouldn't deliver it to our customers until it was ready and so we didn't. Those are tough decisions

Do not ever compromise your personal values … because it's much harder to re-establish them than it is to establish them the first time around.

to make, especially when hundreds of millions to billions of euros are invested in an activity and your decision is: 'I am not going to do it. I will take the impact on the business. I am not going to do it until it delivers the right customer experience.'

Such a decision is a reflection of your business values and of your personal values. If your team sees you being true to your values and knows you will take that approach on big decisions, then you provide clear decision-making criteria for your team to live by, and you lead along a clearly established path. Your people will never come back and question your values. When they are making their decisions on a daily basis, they can use the same value filter for their own decision-making: that leads to more empowered teams, which leads to quicker decisions, and that leads to clarity and efficiency.

Once you have established a 'brand' value for yourself and stated what your personal brand stands for, live up to it, day in and day out. Do not ever compromise your personal values or your brand values, because it's much harder to re-establish them than it is to establish them the first time around. ”

Executive Timeline Sanjiv Ahuja

Early Years	Degree in electrical engineering, Delhi University, India. Masters Degree Columbia University, New York.
1979–1994	**IBM** Various executive roles, including leading IBM's entry into the telecommunications software industry. IBM is a major multinational company, specializing in computer hardware and software, and in providing IT consultancy.
1994–2000	**Bell Communications Research** *President* Bell is the world's largest provider of operations support systems, network software and consulting and engineering services to the telecommunications industry.
2000–2002	Venture capital businesses
2003–2004	**Orange Group** *Chief Operating Officer*
2004–present	*Chief Executive Officer*
2006–present	**Cadbury Schweppes** *Director*

Emotion is a valuable tool in business. While it is undoubtedly effective in getting your point across, over-using it decreases its impact. Use it sparingly, however, and it is a potent addition to your armoury.

10a Use Emotion Sparingly

Sir David Michels

Former Group Chief Executive, *Hilton Group*

“I began my career path as a waiter in Simpson’s-in-the-Strand before becoming an assistant to the Assistant Controller in a hotel called the Mostyn in Oxford Street. I spent fifteen years in sales and marketing with the hotel chain Grand Metropolitan, five of which were spent in America. My time with Grand Metropolitan was an instant success that took fifteen years. I finished there as Worldwide Sales and Marketing Director about the time Sir Maxwell Joseph died and the company bought Intercontinental. I then spent ten years with the leisure group Ladbrokes, starting as a Sales Representative for the hotel division, before becoming Managing Director of a gaming machine division for three years, which was fascinating.

Ladbrokes bought Hilton and I became a Senior Vice President of both organizations. I left Ladbrokes in 1981 on 1 April, the same date that I joined the company. There must be a moral in that tale – especially as I returned to Ladbrokes, again on 1 April funnily enough. I left Ladbrokes the first time to become Chief Executive of Stakis plc, an ailing hotel chain in Scotland, with a wonderful brand name and some marvellous people. We moved that company from a market cap of £24 million and sold it to Hilton nine years later for £1.8 billion – so a modicum of success there. I returned to Hilton Ladbrokes, and three years ago became CEO of the Hilton Group.

Sir David Michels

Former Group Chief Executive, *Hilton Group*

Sir David Michels left the Hilton Group in 2006.

In business a manager can get excited only so many times a year in order to be effective; and when it happens everything has to quake. Use it once a week and eventually everyone will ignore you.

Emotion is a valuable tool in business, but it has to be used sparingly. I use emotion, whether in anger or fear or anything else that seems appropriate, but in business a manager can get excited only so many times a year in order for the emotion to be effective; and when it happens everything has to quake. Use it once a week and eventually everyone will ignore you. However, there are occasions, particularly when dealing with people who don't know you, when the use of emotion can have a powerful effect.

I was on the Board of Arcadia – the company that was sold two or three years ago to the entrepreneur and retailer Philip Green. The Board was meeting to decide whether to sell the company for a price vastly higher than it had been when most of us had started. Stuart Rose, currently of Marks & Spencer, was the Chief Executive who had been brought in to save the company, and we had a great Chairman called Adam Broadbent. I was simply the Non-executive Director.

At the end of the day the Board has the responsibility for deciding whether to sell the company on, and whether we are doing the right thing for the shareholders. You can't take a straw poll. I wouldn't say the decision was near the cut, but we were fairly certain we needed to sell, when, in the middle of the meeting, Stuart Rose stood up and said: 'I can get us an extra dividend.' The extra dividend was 7p or 8p added on to the share price, but Stuart didn't say it in a calm tone of voice; he was emphatic: 'I CAN GET IT.' It became an emotional challenge. Now I admired Stuart enormously, but he was due to get a huge amount of money anyhow. He said: 'I can go to Philip Green; I can talk him through it and I can get that extra 7p,' multiplied by however many tens of million shares it was. We were all a bit doubtful because it was definitely an emotional outburst rather than a fine money calculation. Off went Stuart. We received a call to come back to the boardroom about six hours later, and Stuart came back with his 7p.

Stuart Rose and Philip Green are both hard businessmen, and although I wasn't there and I didn't witness the conversation I'm absolutely sure it was not a scientific agreement based upon the value, because there was no possibility of a scientific agreement: the Board had more or less reached that conclusion already. It was an emotional response of the 'I have to have this sort of deal, or it won't be done' ilk. Obviously, or willingly – we'll never know – Philip Green was prepared to buy that argument. It is an agreement that could never have been achieved by letter; it could never have been agreed by calculator. That kind of agreement can only be reached using real emotion.

Emotion is a tool you bring out of the toolbox only very, very rarely in business, and its use is instinctive.

I remember trying to inspire one hundred General Managers to stick by a brand name that was not yet famous throughout the UK. The brand was Stakis. I had never used emotion in that way before and I would never do it again. I found myself quoting Martin Luther King and genuinely, without planning, I had tears in my eyes because I really cared. It is not something that you can rehearse unless you're a full-time actor, and that I'm not. I'm trying to be a full-time businessman – and that takes up enough of the time. I really did care; the Managers knew I cared and the impact ricocheted, absolutely ricocheted around the room. On that occasion it was pure emotion. I managed to transfer it from the platform to the audience and back again, which inspired me more. When you can get that degree of electricity purely from emotion, it works.

Emotion is a tool you bring out of the toolbox only very, very rarely in business, and its use is instinctive. It's not something that you can plan to use, or something that should be part of your upfront arsenal. It's just something that's there; something in your brain just ticks and says: 'Use the emotional card.' Be aware, however, that it's the joker in the pack; it's a card you can play only once every fifty-two times.

Often the bigger you get in business, the greater the temptation to ask others' opinion about decisions that need to be made. But beware of putting too much faith in committees and consultants. While they are there to assist the individual in making the right decision, they are not there to make the decision for them.

ob Beware of Committees

It seems that the further a leader progresses in business, and the more one grows in life, the more frequently one wants to ask other people their opinions, get everybody on board, have all the specialists come in, and get all the outside help that can be found.

The tendency to want to consult reminds me of when I was a fairly junior employee at Grand Metropolitan, now called Diageo. Its Chairman at that time, and the founder of the company, was Sir Maxwell Joseph. He did everything on his own. He made all his decisions, and would then phone up his managers to tell them what he'd decided to do. He bought three hotels in Paris one day – the Grande, the Maurice and the Prince De Gaulle – a deal in today's money of at least £250 million. Then he called both me and my boss at the time to say: 'I've just bought three hotels in Paris – will you take care of them?' We were both so scared of him that it was the next day before we had the courage to ask which they were. We almost headed to Paris without knowing the names of the hotels.

Eventually, having bought the freehold of some eighty or ninety hotels, Max must have given in to the enormous pressure coming from his fellow Directors, because he decided to buy the next hotel by committee. The hotel in question was the Royal Manhattan in New York on 44th Street and Lexington, which, thirty years ago, was a terrible place. It was a big hotel, with 1300 bedrooms, and was being sold for a lot of money for the time. The Sales Director and the Finance Director went out there, we asked seventeen consultants to give their opinions, and we did surveys of the customers and the area. Then Max bought the hotel.

It was the only single hotel he ever bought for about $100 million and sold at a loss two years later for $12 million. That doesn't mean that no decision should ever be taken by committee, but it does mean that if a guy has an enormous talent for something – in Max's case, an instinct for property – he doesn't need to ask dozens of other people.

There is a famous story about Sir Maxwell Joseph that I can 99 per cent verify. He was Chairman and Chief Executive, and any other important title in the 1970s. The 1970s were the time of good corporate governance. People knew how to spell it, but they weren't doing it: they knew the words existed and were just beginning to look at the concept. Sir Max had a main Board of about fifteen people. One day he went to the normal Board meeting and informed everybody that he was going to buy – I can't remember the exact figure – about £50 million worth of Savoy shares, which was a lot of money in those days. He just mentioned it in passing. The Board decided for the first time ever to flex a bit of muscle, and found the courage – I don't know where from – to vote 15:1 against Max going out with the company's money to buy Savoy shares. The vote was duly recorded, yet about an hour and a half after the Board meeting Max went out and bought the shares anyway. True story? Probably...

I'm not sure there is a moral in this tale that is applicable today, but the end of the story is that he turned that money over twice in six months. That doesn't mean there shouldn't be good corporate governance – of course there should be. It doesn't mean that you can go against your Board today; that is an impossibility. However, it does mean that 15:1 is not always right.

Committees and consultants are there to assist the individual in making the right decision – but they are not there to make the decision for the individual. If you have reached a stage in your career where you are being paid to make a decision, make one. ”

Executive Timeline Sir David Michels

Early career	Graduate – London Hotel School
	Grand Metropolitan *Worldwide Marketing Director* Spent fifteen years with the company, mainly in sales and marketing roles.
1981	**Ladbroke Group plc**
	Sales and Marketing Director – Ladbroke Hotels
1983	*Managing Director* – Ladbroke Leisure Division
1985	*Managing Director* – Ladbroke Hotels
1987	**Hilton International** *Senior Vice President, Sales and Marketing* Appointed following acquisition of Hilton International by Ladbroke Group.
1989	**Hilton UK** *Deputy Chairman*
	Hilton International *Executive Vice President*
1991	**Stakis plc** *Chief Executive Officer* Steered the group to a leading position in the UK hospitality sector.
1999	Stakis acquired by Hilton Group.
March 1999	**Hilton Group (formerly Ladbroke Group)** Joined the board.
April 1999	**Hilton International** *Chief Executive*
2000–2006	**Hilton Group** *Group Chief Executive* Responsible for Hilton Group/Hilton International Hotels (UK) Ltd/Scandic Hotels AB.
2006	Received International Hotel Investment Forum's Lifetime Achievement Award

Alongside attention to detail, direct personal involvement and communication with all stakeholders is crucial to leaders running a company. However, giving people the freedom to run their business units autonomously, without interference, is also essential.

11 Attention to Detail

Sir Martin Sorrell

Group Chief Executive, *WPP*

“I was born in 1945 and went to Haberdashers’ Aske’s School in a Jewish community in northwest London. I was granted a place at Cambridge University, but before I went there I had a summer job at the journal Management Today, so I’m a frustrated journalist really. At Cambridge I read economics.

I went straight to Harvard Business School after that and had a summer job in the UK at Marks & Spencer. After graduating from Harvard in 1969 I worked for Glendenning Associates – a marketing consultancy in Westport, Connecticut. Then I joined Mark McCormack at IMG – the sports and lifestyle marketing and management company. At the time they managed Arnold Palmer, Gary Player, Jack Nicklaus, Jean-Claude Killy, Jean Shrimpton – the light of my life – and all sorts of other interesting people.

After that I joined James Gulliver of the Argyll Group as a Personal Financial Advisor, which meant that I carried his bags and was his gofer. He made an investment in Saatchi & Saatchi: I met Maurice and Charles Saatchi and became their Chief Financial Officer for nine years. Following my attack of andropause in 1985, I decided to go into business for myself – hence WPP. I’m Chief Executive of WPP, one of the world’s largest communications services companies, and it’s a job I’ve been enjoying for twenty years.

Sir Martin Sorrell

Group Chief Executive, *WPP*

I think of the company as being mine, so to have an understanding and knowledge of what's going on inside it is critically important.

A lot of people think they can annoy me or upset me by calling me a micro-manager, but I don't take it as an insult. I think it's a compliment. Attention to detail is critically important. Part of my tendency in this area is due to the fact that I started the company and therefore suffer from 'Founder's Disease'. WPP is very much my baby – or at least I regard it as being my baby – despite the fact that I own a relatively low proportion of the equity. I think of the company as being mine, so to have an understanding and knowledge of what's going on inside it is critically important.

At Saatchi & Saatchi Maurice and Charles Saatchi moved away from the detail of their business. They believed in what they called the 'min-aggro' route, which meant minimum aggravation. This meant that the Directors thought about things, and had people to delegate to, such as Tim Bell on the professional side of the business (the best client man that I've ever come across) and myself on the financial and administrative side. The interesting thing is that if Directors pull too far away from their business and stop exhibiting a true understanding, it is unlikely that they will get back into it.

Like everything in life, management is about balance, but I think I would always err on the side of being involved in the detail and micro-management. If you asked what my central function is and what I should focus on, I would say that my priority is to get the very best people for the business, which we run as fifteen units or operating 'tribes'.

At the same time I need to be involved to some extent with clients and with our people. If I'm not involved, the clients turn around and say: 'You're not interested.' If I'm over-involved with staff, the people running the day-to-day business will say: 'You've hired me to run the business, so let me do it.' Management involves continual stress and strain, and is not easy. Managing and being involved with the clients and people who are the heart of our business is terribly important.

The same principle applies to share-owners. If you isolate yourself from them and say: 'I'm not going to visit Boston or London or wherever they are,' the leadership becomes increasingly isolated. That's not just true of the share-owning community, it's true of everything.

The worst thing you can do is isolate yourself from the Press. When the dreaded journalist calls from the dreaded journal, any journal, and is going to write a nasty piece – a 'minus ten' piece – on WPP (there are often 'minus ten' pieces on WPP), I know that if I speak personally to the journalist, it will make a positive difference: he or she will write a piece that is a minus

If someone were to ask me what I would like as my epitaph or in my obituary, it would say that I was somebody who not only founded a business, but also managed to run it on a considerable scale.

eight or a minus nine. If I don't speak to the journalist, the result could be a minus eleven or a minus twelve. It's no good handing the responsibility to a bevy of communications people inside the company or to an agency. Direct involvement and direct communication is critically important.

Aligned to this belief is another important lesson that I've learned. If someone were to ask me what I would like as my epitaph or in my obituary, it would say that I was somebody who not only founded a business, but also managed to run it on a considerable scale. Starting something is only half of it. It's a bit like buying a company and then not being able to run it. It's very easy to spend money in acquisition, particularly in buoyant economic conditions like the ones we experienced in the 1990s. It's very difficult to make a company operate effectively, and extract the synergies and implement the strategy. Therefore, attention to detail is very important. ”

Executive Timeline Sir Martin Sorrell

1968	Graduated from Harvard Business School.
1968–1969	**Glendenning Associates** US-based marketing consultancy in Westport, Connecticut
1970–1974	**Mark McCormack Organization** Managed the business affairs of sports personalities.
1975–1977	**James Gulliver Associates** Worked personally for James Gulliver.
1977–1984	**Saatchi & Saatchi** *Group Finance Director* Saatchi & Saatchi is an advertising agency group.
1986–present	**WPP Group** *Group Chief Executive* WPP is one of the world's largest communications services companies. Major brands include advertising agencies JWT Company, Ogilvy & Mather Worldwide and Y&R.

Perhaps because I view life as one long learning process I have always believed that the way you learn is by having really smart people around you. If they're smarter than you, even better.

12 Populate Your Inner Circle With Experts

Laura Tyson

Former Dean of *London Business School*, and Former White House National Economic Adviser

My Career

“The most important part of this story, begins with my finding economics as my professional interest in college, knowing from early on that I wanted to have a career which was primarily based in academics. So my career really, if you look at it historically, has been exactly that: it's been as a professional economist. I made a decision to get a PhD in economics at MIT, it was a great opportunity, it sort of influenced everything else.

From that degree, I was able to get positions in a number of prestigious institutions of higher education, Princeton University for a few years, went on leave to the University of California at Berkeley, decided to stay at the University of California at Berkeley, because I felt more at home with the interdisciplinary nature of their research.

I knew that I wanted to get engaged in bringing economics out of the classroom, into the world of public policy where I stayed in academia, so I then got involved in a number of consulting projects with the Royal Bank, with a number of governmental commissions on global trade and competitiveness. Those were very important choices on my part, because they embedded me in policy networks, which essentially is the way I ultimately ended up in Washington. It wasn't so much that I was engaged with candidate's running campaigns – I had not actually been very politically active

– but I had been very policy active over a decade, and doing a series of consulting special projects for state governments, for federal government, for international organizations.

I took leave to go to Washington, served in two positions there, the Chair of the Council of Economic Advisers for two years. And then something, which sounds the same but is not quite the same, the Chair of the National Economic Council. The Council of Economic Advisors is advisory: it basically sits at the table with all of the other economic policy making institutions of the US Government. It has a seat at the table. The National Economic Council coordinates all economic policy making, so in the second two years, I was in a much more political job, much more bringing people together, getting position papers for the President together. So it was a very interesting opportunity for me, because it took me out of the advisory, and put me much more into the political side of the world.

Then I had the opportunity after I left, I went back to the University of California, pretty clear I no longer wanted to be just a professor, and I was asked to become the Dean of the Business School. I thought that was a good combination of policy and administrative experience, which I certainly had from Washington, and would give me room to continue to teach as a professor. And then four years later I was asked by London Business School did I want to take on the Deanship there.

Laura Tyson

Former Dean of *London Business School* and Former White House National Economic Adviser

Laura Tyson stood down as the Dean of London Business School at the end of 2006, and is now a professor at the Haas School of Business at the University of California Berkeley.

I think it's very important for people at the head of organizations not to be afraid of having the smartest people in the room, and indeed people who are smarter than they are. This really has to do with recognising what your competence is, and what you need around you.

This is a lesson about the people you bring in to work with you, and the importance of getting the very best people you can. Even if in some cases they have such strong reputations that you might think they're going to compete with you for reputational benefit, in fact, they're going to help you.

Perhaps because I view life as one long learning process I have always believed that the way you learn is by having really smart people around you. If they're smarter than you, even better.

I was brought in to chair a council of economic advisors. Normally, the distinction between the Chair – Chairwoman, Chairman, I use the word Chair – and the two members, is a pretty important one. So the Chairman – the head – is usually by general reputation, and by going into rooms, considered to be quite a significant leader relative to the two members.

My view was to try to bring in members who were at the absolute top of their profession. Indeed, the two members that I brought in were considered to be top-notch in their fields. I felt that to have such people around me would allow me to do my job better, and would also allow the institution to more easily achieve its mission. I didn't draw any distinction hierarchically between myself and them. One of these individuals went on to win the Nobel Prize in economics while another became the Vice Chairman of the Federal Reserve, so I think I chose pretty well.

When you need individuals of that level of accomplishment, you also have to think about ways to engage them. To my mind, in many cases that means having no hierarchy at all. Essentially it's a team of equals.

I brought these people into every room with me; they were not just my deputies, they were my co-equals. I created that atmosphere. The benefits were two-fold: I got huge reputational benefits for running the council like that, for being able to attract such talent, and for treating them without any sense of hierarchy at all. Second, the organization I led – the advice we gave to the President – was as good as it could possibly be because I had brought in this level of expertise.

I think it's very important for people at the head of organizations not to be afraid of having the smartest people in the room, and indeed people who are smarter than they are. This really has to do with recognizing what your competence is, and what you need around you. But when you need individuals of that level of accomplishment, you also have to think about ways to engage them. To my mind, in many cases that means having no hierarchy at all. Essentially it's a team of equals. ”

Executive Timeline Laura Tyson

Early years	**Princeton University** *Assistant Professor, Department of Economics* **UC Berkeley** *Professor, Department of Economics* *Director of Research, Berkeley Roundtable on the International Economy*
1993–1995	**President's Council of Economic Advisors** *Chairman*
1990–1992	**UC Berkeley** *Director, Institute of International Studies*
1995–1996	**National Economic Council** *Chairman* First woman to hold post
1997–2001	**Law and Economics Consulting Group** *Principal*
1998–2001	**UC Berkeley** *Dean, Haas School of Business*
1990–2001	**UC Berkeley** *Professor, Haas School of Business*
2002–2006	**London Business School** *Dean*
2007–present	**University of California Berkeley** *Professor, Haas School of Business*
1997–present	**Ameritech Corp.** *Director until acquired by AT&T in 1999* **Morgan Stanley** *Director* **Eastman Kodak Company** *Director*